Holiday Magic Books

Presidents' Day

MAGIC

by James W. Baker
pictures by George Overlie

Lerner Publications Company Minneapolis

To my brother, Bill, and his wife, Vivian, who elected to encourage and support me over the years in my bid for the high office of magic.

Library of Congress Cataloging-in-Publication Data
Baker, James W., 1926-
    Presidents day magic.

    (Holiday magic books)
    Summary: Explains how to perform magic tricks
revolving around a Presidents' Day theme.
    1. Tricks—Juvenile literature. 2. Presidents—
United States—Juvenile literature. 3. Holidays—
United States—Juvenile literature. [1. Magic
tricks. 2. Presidents] I. Overlie, George, ill.
II. Title. III. Series: Baker, James W., 1926-
Holiday magic books.
GV1548.B344 1989   793.8   88-8341
ISBN 0-8225-2232-2 (lib. bdg.)

Manufactured in the United States of America

1 2 3 4 5 6 7 8 9 10 98 97 96 95 94 93 92 91 90 89

CONTENTS

INTRODUCTION

In the middle of cold and dreary February, two of the most famous presidents of the United States —George Washington and Abraham Lincoln— were born. To honor these men, as well as the other past presidents, most states celebrate Presidents' Day. You may get a holiday from school or you may spend the school day learning about the lives and accomplishments of the past leaders of the United States.

If you are at school on Presidents' Day, you might read the Gettysburg Address or reenact the story of Washington crossing the Delaware. But if you are at home, your sisters, brothers, and friends will vote for a Presidents' Day magic show.

You'll be a sure winner and brighten a February day when your audience elects you to lead them through these magic tricks.

HOW IT LOOKS

After you write a prediction, lay nine cards out on the table, each with the name of a president and his party written on it. Tell your friend to make certain "jumps" with a magic penny. At the end of each jump—even though you have your back turned and can't see where the magic penny landed—tell your friend the name of a card it did not land on. Tell him to remove that card. After doing this eight times and removing eight cards, your friend is left with one card, the one you had predicted.

HOW TO MAKE IT

1. For this trick, you will need nine index cards. On each card, write the name and party of a different president. Lay the cards on the table as shown (**Figure 1**).

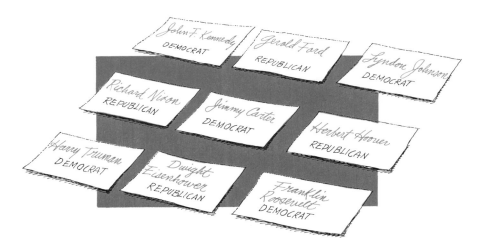

2. You will also need a slip of paper, a pencil, and a bright, shiny, "magic penny."

9

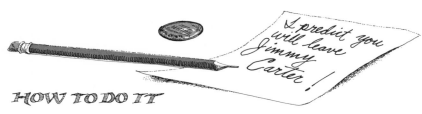

HOW TO DO IT

1. Without letting your friend see what you are writing on the slip of paper, write "I predict you will leave Jimmy Carter." Fold up the slip of paper and set it aside in plain view. Tell your friend it is your prediction.

2. With your back turned so you can't see what he's doing, have your friend put the magic penny on any card with the name of a Democratic president. The choice is his. Explain that you are going to instruct him to make a certain number of "jumps," but he is free to "jump" anywhere he wishes. A "jump" consists of moving the magic penny to the next card or empty space above, below, or to either side, but not diagonally. Again, the choice is his.

3. Give your friend these instructions:

1. Take away Herbert Hoover.
2. Jump seven times. Your penny did not land on John F. Kennedy. Take the Kennedy card away.
3. Jump four times. You did not land on Franklin Roosevelt. Take Roosevelt away.
4. Jump six times. You are not on Harry Truman. Take Truman away.
5. Jump five times. You are not on Dwight Eisenhower. Take Eisenhower away.
6. Jump twice. You did not land on Richard Nixon. Take Nixon away.
7. Jump once. You are not on Lyndon Johnson. Take Johnson away.
8. Jump seven times. You did not land on Gerald Ford. Take Ford away.

4. Now there should be one card left on the table—Jimmy Carter. Ask your friend to open and read your prediction.

HOW IT LOOKS

You write down a prediction and then show a list of presidents in helter-skelter order. Turn your back and give your friend some instructions. He ends up drawing a ring around the name of a certain president, the very one you had predicted.

HOW TO MAKE IT

For this trick, you will need a slip of paper, a pencil, and a list of 35 presidents. Choose 35 from the list of 41 presidents on page 45 and write them down in random order. Although there must be 35 presidents on your list, don't tell this to your friend. Just say this is a list of "some of the presidents."

HOW TO DO IT

1. Without letting your friend see, write down the name of the 17th president on the list. Fold your prediction and set it on the table.

2. Give the list of presidents to your friend and turn your back so that you can't see what he's doing.

3. Tell your friend to cross out five to ten names at the beginning of the list without skipping any. The choice of how many to cross out is his. Then have him cross out one to five names from the end of the list without skipping any (**Figure 1**).

figure 1.

6 crossed out at the beginning of the list

WOODROW WILSON
GROVER CLEVELAND
JAMES MONROE
HARRY TRUMAN
JOHN TYLER
CALVIN COOLIDGE
THOMAS JEFFERSON
RICHARD NIXON
FRANKLIN PIERCE
THEODORE ROOSEVELT
ANDREW JACKSON
HERBERT HOOVER
RONALD REAGAN
ABRAHAM LINCOLN
WARREN HARDING
JOHN F. KENNEDY

your prediction → JOHN ADAMS

FRANKLIN ROOSEVELT
GEORGE WASHINGTON
JAMES POLK
GERALD FORD
JAMES GARFIELD
ZACHARY TAYLOR
JAMES MADISON
WILLIAM McKINLEY
JIMMY CARTER
ULYSSES S. GRANT
MILLARD FILLMORE
BENJAMIN HARRISON
WILLIAM HARRISON
JOHN QUINCY ADAMS
GEORGE BUSH
CHESTER ARTHUR

2 crossed out at the end of the list

LYNDON JOHNSON
ANDREW JOHNSON

figure 2.

27
↱ *"uncrossed names"*

2 + 7 = ⑨

your friend's resulting number ↰

4. Remind your friend that you have no way of knowing how many "uncrossed" names are left in the middle. Have him count the "uncrossed" names and add the two digits of this number together to get his resulting number, as shown. (**Figure 2**).

5. Ask your friend to count name by name from the top of the "uncrossed" section to the name at his resulting number and put a small dot beside it.

6. Have him go back and count the names he crossed out at the bottom of the list. Then have him count that number of names down from the pencil dot, circling the name on which he finishes counting (**Figure 3**).

7. When he reads your prediction, he will discover that you correctly predicted the president's name he would circle.

figure 3.

~~WOODROW WILSON~~
~~GROVER CLEVELAND~~
~~JAMES MONROE~~
~~HARRY TRUMAN~~
~~JOHN TYLER~~
~~CALVIN COOLIDGE~~
1 THOMAS JEFFERSON
2 RICHARD NIXON
3 FRANKLIN PIERCE
4 THEODORE ROOSEVELT
5 ANDREW JACKSON
6 HERBERT HOOVER
7 RONALD REAGAN
8 ABRAHAM LINCOLN

dot ⟶ • 9 WARREN HARDING
JOHN F. KENNEDY
⟨JOHN ADAMS⟩
FRANKLIN ROOSEVELT
GEORGE WASHINGTON
JAMES POLK
GERALD FORD
JAMES GARFIELD
ZACHARY TAYLOR
JAMES MADISON
WILLIAM McKINLEY
JIMMY CARTER
ULYSSES S. GRANT
MILLARD FILLMORE
BENJAMIN HARRISON
WILLIAM HARRISON
JOHN QUINCY ADAMS
GEORGE BUSH
CHESTER ARTHUR
~~LYNDON JOHNSON~~
~~ANDREW JOHNSON~~

PROFESSOR PHANTOM'S PRESIDENTS

HOW IT LOOKS

Show a list of the 41 presidents of the United States to the audience and ask a volunteer to choose any one of the 41. You then call your friend Professor Phantom. He immediately tells the volunteer which president she chose.

professor's list

HOW TO MAKE IT

For this trick, you will need two lists of the 41 presidents, as shown on page 45.

HOW TO DO IT

You and your friend—Professor Phantom—must work out a special signaling system ahead of time.

1. Let your friend know when you will be calling. He must have the list of presidents by his phone.

2. To begin, tell your audience that you know a professor who can read people's minds.

3. Show the list of presidents to your audience and have a volunteer select one of the presidents. Then call your friend on the phone.

4. When he answers, you say, "Hello, is Professor Phantom there?" That is the signal for your friend to slowly say: "One through 10? . . . 11 through 20? . . . 21 through 30? . . . 31 through 41? . . ." Since you know which president was selected, you know which group the selected president was in. You interrupt your friend as he is saying the correct group by saying something like, "Put the professor on the line please."

For example: if you interrupt when your friend says "21 through 30?" he will know which group of ten the selected president is in.

5. Immediately your friend begins slowly naming those ten presidents.

For example: "Arthur...Cleveland...Harrison...Cleveland...McKinley...Roosevelt...Taft..." etc.

6. Once again, the instant he names the selected president, you interrupt him by saying something like, "Professor Phantom, I want you to talk to someone." This lets him know which president was selected. You immediately hand the phone to the volunteer who selected the president.

7. Then the so-called Professor Phantom says in his most mysterious voice, "I believe that you chose President So-and-so."

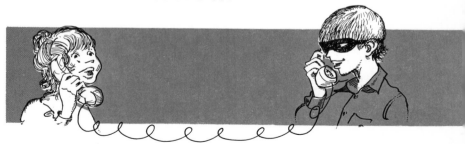

THE RIGHT ABE LINCOLN

HOW IT LOOKS

The audience chooses one penny from a batch of eight or nine pennies, each with a different date. They will remember which one was chosen by remembering its date. The chosen penny is tossed into a paper bag with all the other pennies while you have your back turned. You reach into the bag and bring out the chosen penny which is identified by its date.

20

HOW TO MAKE IT

For this trick, you will need a paper bag and eight or nine pennies, each with a different date.

HOW TO DO IT

1. While your back is turned, have someone pick one of the pennies out of the bag containing eight or nine pennies.
2. Have everyone examine the penny, check its date, and hold it pressed between their palms for a few seconds while concentrating on the date. Then pass it on.
3. Have the last person toss the chosen coin back into the paper bag with the other pennies.
4. You turn around, reach into the bag, and pick out the chosen coin, which is identified by its date. You have chosen the right Abe Lincoln.

Secret: You had everyone examine the coin, hold it pressed between their palms, and concentrate on its date. This was done to make the chosen coin warmer than the others. When you reach into the bag, it is easy to pick out the warmer coin from the other, colder ones.

INDESTRUCTIBLE
GEORGE WASHINGTON

HOW IT LOOKS

Hand a friend a dollar bill and four plain pieces of paper the same size as the dollar. While your back is turned, have her lay the dollar—with George Washington's picture facing up—and the four slips of paper in a row on the table in any order. Have her move the slips of paper and the dollar bill a certain number of times in any direction she chooses and tear up certain pieces.

Miraculously, she tears up the four slips of paper but not the dollar bill, proving that George Washington is indestructible.

HOW TO MAKE IT

For this trick, you will need a dollar bill and four slips of paper that are the same size as the dollar bill.

HOW TO DO IT

1. Give the dollar bill and the four pieces of paper to your friend. Turn your back so you can't see what she's doing during the trick.

2. Ask your friend to arrange the dollar and the slips of paper in a row on the table (**Figure 1**). She may put the dollar any place in the row.

3. Have her rearrange the pieces of paper by "moves." To make a "move," she will switch the position of the dollar bill with the slip of paper on either side of it. If the dollar bill is at the end of the row, there will, of course, be a piece of paper on only one side of it, and therefore only one way to "move."

4. Have your friend note the position of the dollar bill (first, second, third, fourth, or fifth) in the row. She may count from *either* end.

figure 1.

dollar bill in
third position

5. To begin, ask your friend to make the same number of "moves" as the bill's position in the row. For example, if the dollar bill is third in the row, she will "move" it three times.
6. Then have her make two more "moves" with the dollar bill. Ask her to tear up the pieces of paper at each end of the row, telling her you feel sure these are not the dollar bill.
7. Ask her to make one more "move" with the dollar bill and tear up the slip of paper on the far left, since it is not the dollar bill.
8. Ask her to "move" one last time and tear up the slip on the left once more.
9. There will be one piece of paper left—the dollar bill bearing the picture of the indestructible George Washington.

ABE

VERSUS

GEORGE

HOW IT LOOKS

Using a one-dollar bill—George Washington—and a five-dollar bill—Abraham Lincoln—you roll them onto a pencil. Lincoln, who was behind Washington, is now in front of him.

For this trick, you will need a one-dollar bill, a five-dollar bill, and a long pencil.

HOW TO DO IT

1. Place the one-dollar bill on top of the five-dollar bill on a table as shown (**Figure 1**).

figure 1.

2. Ask a friend to hold down the one-dollar bill with her finger on the edge farthest from the five-dollar bill, as shown.

3. Beginning at the lower edge, roll both bills together tightly around the pencil and keep on rolling until you reach your friend's finger.

4. With your friend's finger still on the top edge, you slowly unroll the bills.

5. Magically the two bills have changed places. The five-dollar bill—Lincoln—is now on top of the one-dollar bill—Washington.

WHICH PRESIDENT?

HOW IT LOOKS

You leave the room while your assistant lets the audience choose nine index cards from a pack of 41 cards of the presidents. Your assistant arranges the nine cards on the table. Someone in the audience selects one of the nine presidents. You come back into the room and immediately tell the group which president was selected even though you were out of the room and no one has spoken to you since you returned.

For this trick, you will need 41 index cards, each with the name of a different president written on it. You can use the same cards as used in AT THE DROP OF A HAND. You will also need an assistant who will signal to you which card was chosen without saying a single word.

HOW TO DO IT

1. Leave the room while your assistant has the audience choose nine presidential cards.
2. Your assistant arranges the cards on the table in three rows of three cards each and has a volunteer choose one of the cards.

figure 1.

3. You and your assistant mentally view the cards as being number 1 through 9 as shown (**Figure 1**). Of course, there are no numbers on the cards. When you return to the room, you steal a glance at your assistant's hand which is holding the remaining 32 cards, those not used in the trick.

4. She signals you by holding her thumb on the pack of cards at the same relative position as the selected presidential card (**Figure 2**).

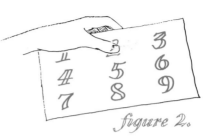

figure 2.

For example: your assistant signals that the card selected was John F. Kennedy, the card in the Number 2 position (**Figure 3**).

figure 3.

selected card

This trick can be repeated one or two times, but don't overdo it or the audience might catch on.

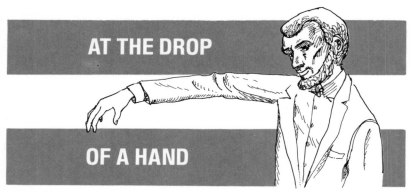

AT THE DROP

OF A HAND

HOW IT LOOKS

You show the audience a pack of 41 index cards with the names of the United States presidents written on them. Turn the cards over so the presidents' names are facedown, shuffle the cards, and have a volunteer choose one. Put the chosen card back on top of the pack. Cut the pack several times, losing the chosen card in the pack. Turn the cards faceup with the presidents' names showing and put them into piles of five or six cards each.

As you hold the volunteer's wrist, move her hand over the piles of cards (Figure 1). When she comes to the right pile—the one containing the chosen card—drop her hand down on the pile. Separate the cards in that pile and, holding her wrist, move her hand over the individual cards. Then, when you drop her hand, it lands right on the presidential card she chose.

figure 1.

HOW TO MAKE IT

For this trick, you will need 41 index cards, each with the name of a different president written on it. You can use the same cards as used in WHICH PRESIDENT.

HOW TO DO IT

1. Make sure you know the name of the president on the bottom card: Abraham Lincoln, for example.
2. Have a volunteer choose a card from the shuffled pack as described in HOW IT LOOKS.
3. Have the chosen card put back on top of the facedown deck. Cut off about half of the cards from the bottom of the deck and drop them on the top of the deck, burying the chosen card in the middle. This will place the Abraham Lincoln card on top of the selected card.

4. Cut the cards several times. (There's almost no chance of Abraham Lincoln and the selected card getting separated from each other.) Tell the volunteer that her selected card is now hopelessly lost in the pack.

5. Turn the cards faceup and spread them out in piles of five or six. The chosen card will be in front of the Abraham Lincoln card (**Figure 2**). Place the piles faceup on the table.

figure 2.

chosen card is in front of Abraham Lincoln

6. Now that you know which card was chosen, the rest of the trick is pure acting, locating the card as described in HOW IT LOOKS.

PICKING A PRESIDENT

HOW IT LOOKS

You correctly predict which of the 41 United States presidents your friend will choose even though she chooses strictly by chance.

HOW TO MAKE IT

For this trick you will need a pencil, two small slips of paper, and a list of the 41 United States presidents, as shown on page 45.

HOW TO DO IT

1. Without letting your friend see, write "You will choose Andrew Johnson" on one slip of paper. Fold the paper and set it out on the table.
2. Give the other slip of paper and the pencil to your friend and tell her that she will be selecting a president totally by chance.

3. Have her write down her favorite number between 50 and 100, then add to it 82. Have her cross out the first digit in the sum and add it to the two-digit number remaining. For example:

Her favorite number 73
Plus . . . . + 82
Equals ₁55
Cross out 1 and then add it . . . + 1
To get her answer 56

4. Next have her subtract her answer from her favorite number between 50 and 100. This will leave her with her final number.

Her favorite number 73
Minus her answer . . . . − 56
To get her final number 17

5. Have her count to the president at her final number. She will see that you correctly predicted the president she selected completely by chance.

If your friend starts with any two-digit number and follows these math steps, her final number will always be 17. Since she would count to the 17th president, Andrew Johnson, your prediction will always be correct. Obviously, you can't perform this trick more than once for the same friend. You can, however, list the presidents in random order rather than in the order in which they served. Your friend will still come up with 17. It would not be Andrew Johnson, the 17th president, but whatever president was listed 17th on the list.

PRESIDENTIAL COINS

HOW IT LOOKS

You correctly predict which of four coins—each bearing the likeness of a president—was chosen by your friend.

HOW TO MAKE IT

You will need four coins—a penny, a nickel, a dime, and a quarter—and four slips of paper.

1. Before showing this trick, secretly write a different prediction on each of the four pieces of paper:

   A. I honestly think you will choose Abe Lincoln.

   B. I declare that you will independently choose Thomas Jefferson.

   C. Frankly, I think you will choose the Roosevelt coin.

   D. I cannot tell a lie; you will choose George Washington.

2. Put each of the predictions in a different pocket and remember which pocket contains which prediction.

3. Begin the trick by asking your friend if he can name the presidents whose pictures appear on the penny, nickel, dime, and quarter. Whether or not he can, toss the four coins on the table and let him have a look.

4. Turn your back and tell your friend to hold one coin in his hand and put the other three in his pocket, without telling you which one he is holding.

5. Turn back around and ask him to open his hand so you can see which coin he selected. When you see the coin, ask him to reach in your pocket and remove the prediction you made before the trick began. Open the pocket so he can reach in and get the prediction, making sure you open the pocket that contains the right prediction.

6. Make sure you get your coins back or else you will have played a trick on yourself.

LIST OF UNITED STATES PRESIDENTS

1. George Washington
2. John Adams
3. Thomas Jefferson
4. James Madison
5. James Monroe
6. John Quincy Adams
7. Andrew Jackson
8. Martin Van Buren
9. William Harrison
10. John Tyler
11. James Polk
12. Zachary Taylor
13. Millard Fillmore
14. Franklin Pierce
15. James Buchanan
16. Abraham Lincoln
17. Andrew Johnson
18. Ulysses S. Grant
19. Rutherford B. Hayes
20. James Garfield
21. Chester Arthur
22. Grover Cleveland
23. Benjamin Harrison
24. Grover Cleveland
25. William McKinley
26. Theodore Roosevelt
27. William Howard Taft
28. Woodrow Wilson
29. Warren Harding
30. Calvin Coolidge
31. Herbert Hoover
32. Franklin Roosevelt
33. Harry Truman
34. Dwight Eisenhower
35. John F. Kennedy
36. Lyndon Johnson
37. Richard Nixon
38. Gerald Ford
39. Jimmy Carter
40. Ronald Reagan
41. George Bush

TRICKS FOR BETTER MAGIC

Here are some simple rules you should keep in mind while learning to perform the tricks in this book.

1. Read the entire trick several times until you thoroughly understand it.
2. Practice the trick alone or in front of a mirror until you feel comfortable doing the trick, then present it to an audience.
3. Learn to perform one trick perfectly before moving on to another trick. It is better to perform one trick well than a half dozen poorly.
4. Work on your "presentation." Make up special "patter" (what you say while doing a trick) that is funny and entertaining. Even the simplest trick becomes magical when it is properly presented.
5. Choose tricks that suit you and your personality. Some tricks will work better for you than others.

Stick with these. *Every* trick is not meant to be performed by *every* magician.

6. Feel free to experiment and change a trick to suit you and your unique personality so that you are more comfortable presenting it.

7. Never reveal the secret of the trick. Your audience will respect you much more if you do not explain the trick. When asked how you did a trick, simply say "by magic."

8. Never repeat a trick for the same audience. If you do, you will have lost the element of surprise and your audience will probably figure out how you did it the second time around.

9. Take your magic seriously, but not yourself. Have fun with magic and your audience will have fun along with you.

ABOUT THE AUTHOR

James W. Baker, a magician for over 30 years, has performed as "Mister Mystic" in hospitals, orphanages, and schools around the world. He is a member of the International Brotherhood of Magicians and the Society of American Magicians, and is author of *Illusions Illustrated*, a magic book for young performers.

From 1951 to 1963, Baker was a reporter for *The Richmond (VA) News Leader*. From 1963 to 1983, he was an editor with the U.S. Information Agency, living in Washington, D.C., India, Turkey, Pakistan, the Philippines, and Tunisia, and traveling in 50 other countries. Today Baker and his wife, Elaine, live in Williamsburg, Virginia, where he performs magic and writes for the local newspaper, *The Virginia Gazette*.

ABOUT THE ARTIST

George Overlie is a talented artist who has illustrated numerous books. Born in the small town of Rose Creek, Minnesota, Overlie graduated from the New York Phoenix School of Design and began his career as a layout artist. He soon turned to book illustration and proved his skill and versatility in this demanding field. For Overlie, fantasy, illusion, and magic are all facets of illustration and have made doing the Holiday Magic books a real delight.